Original title:
Leaves and Letters

Author: Gideon Barrett

ISBN HARDBACK: 978-1-80581-899-1
ISBN PAPERBACK: 978-1-80581-426-9
ISBN EBOOK: 978-1-80581-899-1

Reflections on a Whispers' Journey

In the garden of chit-chat, where gossip grows tall,
An echo of secrets begins to enthrall.
With a laugh and a wink, they dance in the breeze,
Like butterflies teasing, moving with ease.

A notion can flutter, a thought takes a flight,
Spinning round corners, it giggles with delight.
Whispers take off, on a whimsical spree,
Tickling the branches of a storytelling tree.

Oh, the tales that are woven, oh, the laughs that they share,
Like squirrels in a bind, with quite the wild flair.
Each message delivered, yet twisted in jest,
A riddle on branches, we give it our best!

So let's toast to the whispers, both silly and grand,
To the hiccups of humor that drift through the land.
For in every mischief, and every small jest,
Lies a spark of laughter, an unforgettable quest!

Scribbles in the Wind

A gust blew through, oh what a sight,
A paper plane took off in flight.
It looped and twirled, a daring dance,
Till it got stuck in a tree's expanse.

The tree sighed deep, 'Not again, my friend!'
'Your scribbles always seem to bend.'
Rustling pages, a giggle so spry,
As notes were stuck, waving goodbye.

The Archive of Shimmer and Shadow

In a drawer, gems hide away,
With scrawl and doodles that jest and play.
A journal flops, with ink in a pool,
It laughs out loud, 'A messy fool!'

A light flickers, stories unfold,
Of cartoons and chaos, tales of old.
A shadow sneezes, it whispers 'Who knew?'
The archive chuckles, shaking its hue.

Mementos of the Season

A hat with a feather, a shoe full of cheer,
Collecting strange odds, they gather near.
One sock insists it's a treasure rare,
While tangled in twine, it begins to stare.

The winter's whispers tells tales so bright,
Of scarves that tickle and funny flight.
Mementos gather, a giggling heap,
As everyone sorts, their memories leap.

Tales from Under the Bark

Beneath the crust, a squirrel dons specs,
Reading old jokes, pondering the checks.
With acorns as punchlines, and bark as the stage,
His stand-up is wild, full of sage.

A beetle in bowtie brings laughter to all,
With ant and grasshopper, they have a ball.
Underneath layers, old tales are spun,
Whispered in giggles, oh what fun!

The Language of Decaying Borders

In the garden, secrets speak,
Written in a shade of mystique.
Crisp notes flutter, soft and sly,
As the breeze plays a witty lie.

A squirrel scribbles on a bark,
Chasing thoughts, it's quite a lark.
While ants conspire, tiny but grand,
Plotting fun in their little land.

Overhead, the paper plane flies,
Crafted from dreams and silly sighs.
It zigzags like a comic strip,
As laughter teases on its trip.

Manuscripts in the Meadow

In the meadow, tales unfold,
Doodles of buttercups, bright and bold.
Grass blades whisper joyfully low,
As butterflies dance, stealing the show.

A hedgehog pens with a twig,
Drawing portraits, oh so big.
Each stroke is quirky, wild, and funny,
Turnips giggle, bright as honey.

Crickets chirp in rhythmic time,
Writing sonnets, feeling sublime.
A rabbit hops, a calm critique,
While daisies blush, their beauty unique.

Tales Tucked Between Branches

Up in the trees, where mischief thrives,
Chirpy squirrels lead double lives.
With acorns stacked like books in rows,
They tell their tales as laughter flows.

A raccoon wearing spectacles red,
Proofreads scripts from the day's thread.
With every rustle, a giggle bursts,
As nature's voice, it deeply thirsts.

Owls offer wisdom, a cheeky glance,
While tree frogs join the silly dance.
In this great library, a bark and a laugh,
The snippets of joy create their own path.

The Poetry of Verdant Whispers

In the green arms of nature's embrace,
Funny critters find their place.
Chirps and squeaks compose the day,
As leaves chuckle in a playful sway.

A snail drafts lines, but oh so slow,
Pondering if it'll steal the show.
With puns like petals in the sun,
Every word is just so fun!

The wind giggles through the boughs,
As wisdom peeks from hidden cows.
A punchline here, a rhyme so sweet,
Nature's punch, can't be beat!

Inked in Autumn's Embrace

The trees wear a coat that's a bit too bright,
Sending critters scampering left and right.
Squirrels in hats, they prepare for the chill,
While acorns roll out with a mischievous thrill.

With each gust, a dance, the branches sway,
Birds tweet complaints of winter's delay.
A postcard from summer, they can't quite ignore,
But soon they'll be grumbling, wishing for more.

Pages of a Dying Season

The ground's a confetti of colors misplaced,
Nature's confessions are flung in the haste.
Crickets are giggling, they won't take a break,
As twilight whispers, it's time for their flake.

Frogs are debating, “Shall we hop or just croak?”
While spiders weave tales in the fog and the smoke.
Raccoons pull pranks, stealing snacks from the deck,
In this crazy season, there’s always a wreck.

Nature's Script Unfurling

The wind plays a trick with a wave and a shout,
Sending old secrets spilling all about.
Trees spill their gossip, and squirrels take note,
These whispers of past trips they giddily wrote.

A fox dons a scarf that he swiped from the rack,
Strutting through puddles with style, no lack.
The sky shows off clouds that play hide-and-seek,
And nature chuckles, “How quirky and chic!”

Chronicles of the Wind

The breeze tells a tale of forgotten lore,
As it tickles the grass, asking for more.
A cat on the fence pulls a face so grand,
While dandelions giggle, “We don't go as planned!”

Caterpillars gossip, their dreams take to flight,
Writing cheeky sonnets to friends, what a sight!
A parade of oddities, strange and bizarre,
In this wild storybook, you’ll travel afar.

Ciphers in the Glade

In the forest, whispers play,
Squirrels debate in a comical way.
One drops a nut, a grand faux pas,
While another just giggles, 'Ha-ha!'

A raccoon writes scripts in the dirt,
Claims he's an author, but just a flirt.
With every scratch, he thinks he's brilliant,
But really, it's just a mess; how resilient!

The owls snicker from their high throne,
Reading the scripts with a playful tone.
Pen and quill made from twigs and moss,
Their literary game? A total loss!

Gnomes critique each misplaced dot,
Arguing over the silliest thought.
In the glade, laughter intertwines,
While art from nature merrily shines.

Resilience of the Underscore

Beneath the trees, where shadows creep,
Lies a tale that seldom sleeps.
A mushroom thinks it's wise and grand,
But dances awkward, can't quite stand.

The snails trail lines like scribbled prose,
Crafting stories no one knows.
With a flick of slime, they leave a jest,
The slowest authors, they're just the best!

Toadstools gather, forming a club,
Weekly potlucks—what a grub!
Share their dreams, and wobbly cheer,
For who doesn't love a good root beer?

Each resilient laugh, a tale to tell,
In the book of life, all is well.
As twilight dims the leafy floor,
Knock, knock—who's there? Just the underscore!

The Diary of Dappled Light

A sunbeam peeks through branches wide,
Finding secrets it can't abide.
It flickers on a leaf so bright,
Laughing at shadows in mid-flight.

A deer poses like a tourist snap,
With a silly grin, oh what a chap!
It prances past, and in moments bold,
Quoting the sun—yet feeling cold.

Caterpillars in tutus prance,
Hosting a ball, oh what a chance!
With a wiggle and giggle, they take a bow,
While crickets clap; they're in the know.

At dusk, they write a very short lore,
About how fun it was to explore.
In dappled light, with friends all around,
Their laughter echoes, joyful and profound.

Chronicles of Rust and Resilience

In the thicket, where oddballs grow,
Time tells tales we barely know.
A secret stash of forgotten things,
Sings with rust; what laughter brings!

A fox with a hat, stylishly bold,
Claims he's a fashionista of old.
While rabbits giggle, no sense of shame,
The forest snickers at his silly game.

A wise old beaver, slightly frazzled,
Whispers wisdom, as giggles dazzled.
“Build more than dams; build a grand art!”
Raccoons reply with a cheeky heart.

Through cracks and creaks of nature's book,
Life scribbles smiles; just take a look.
In the chronicles written with glee,
Title it all—'Let it be free!'

Calligraphy of the Sky

Clouds doodle in the air,
Wind whispers without a care.
Pigeons flutter, ink on the run,
Sketching tales, oh what fun!

Sunbeams shining with a twist,
Painting rainbows, can't resist.
Each drop is a giggle, oh such cheer,
Nature's postcard, crystal clear!

The Rhythm of Falling

Squirrels dance in a dizzy spree,
Chasing shadows, wild and free.
Acorns tumble, taking a dive,
In the air, the squirrels thrive!

Crisp crunch under tiny toes,
Nature's laughter, joy that flows.
Twisting through the autumn air,
Leaves tumble, a wacky flair!

Stories Beneath the Boughs

Underneath the sprawling trees,
Bugs tell jokes with scuttling ease.
A snail slips in, all shy and slow,
While ladybugs laugh in a row.

Roots gather secrets of the ground,
Whispered giggles all around.
Each shadow a tale, each knot a pun,
Nature's comedy, all in good fun!

Written by Nature’s Hand

The brook babbles in a silly tone,
Crickets chirp a flowery phone.
Each ripple splashes with delight,
Frogs croak rhymes under the night.

Branches sway to a playful beat,
Nature's dance, oh so sweet.
With every twist and turn they play,
A jolly serenade on display!

Chronicle of the Dancing Shadows

In the garden, shadows play,
Twisting, turning, day by day.
A squirrel writes a note with flair,
But loses it to the breezy air.

A prickly cactus joins the fun,
Making jokes with the setting sun.
A lizard laughs, does a little jig,
While crickets sing, oh so big!

The flowers dance in silly sync,
Swaying carefree, winking, blink.
With every wiggle, a giggle's heard,
In this garden, all's absurd!

And so it goes, the shadows' glee,
Chasing breezes, wild and free.
In this tale, laughter prevails,
With a rhythm that never fails.

Scripts in the Embrace of Time

Tick-tock, the clock's a clown,
Wearing big shoes, bouncing around.
Time scribbles jokes on parchment thin,
With every tick, it wears a grin.

A watchful owl with spectacles,
Reads the lines of silly funnels.
It hoots out puns, oh such delight,
Turning minutes into pure light.

The sun delays, a master tease,
With rays that dance in breezy ease.
It dips and dives, a playful sprite,
As shadows twirl to the waning night.

In the realm where minutes play,
Life's absurd in every way.
Scripts unravel, laughter climbs,
In the embrace of wrinkled times.

Ink-Soaked Sunlight

Puddles of ink in sunshine beams,
Doodle-swirls of childish dreams.
A pen rolls off, it makes a dash,
Leaving trails of a splashy splash!

Scribbles grow legs, and run about,
As butterflies join in, no doubt.
The canvas giggles with colors bright,
While rainbows play hide-and-seek with light.

A paper airplane takes to the skies,
With scribbled notes and little lies.
It loops and twirls, a daring flight,
Chasing clouds, laughing with delight.

And as the sun dips down to sleep,
Inks blend, and shadows leap.
A canvas full of joyful mess,
In a world where words confess.

Voices Carried by the Gales

Gusts giggle like cheeky jesters,
Carrying tales of past investors.
Whispers bounce on breezy wings,
As the sky wears its laughter rings.

A kite floats high, full of sass,
Disputes with birds who try to pass.
They squawk in jest, sharing a chat,
As the warm wind sends a friendly pat.

In every nook, a secret song,
Echoes of laughter where we belong.
The world twirls in wind-draft cheer,
With every gust, a ticklish sneer.

And when the sun sets, gales still play,
Entwining night with tales of the day.
In a cacophony of joy so grand,
Life's melody dances, hand in hand.

Whispers of Fluttering Pages

In the breeze they do a dance,
With twirls and twirls, they take a chance.
A paper hat flies off my head,
Oh, where it lands? I'll never tread.

A gust of wind, a playful tease,
The notes go swirling, oh what a breeze!
They giggle softly as they sway,
Creating chaos in such a funny way.

Behind the tree, an acorn pranks,
It rolls around, the busy banks.
What ruffled sounds beneath my feet,
A crunchy symphony, can't be beat!

So here we sit, with grins so wide,
As mischief blooms, we cannot hide.
With every flip and flutter close,
They tell tales, oh, they're quite the hosts!

Ink and Petals in the Wind

A droplet falls from pen to ground,
Inked petals scatter all around.
They whirl and giggle, make a mess,
As if to say, 'Oh, what a dress!'

Daffodils giggle, quite bemused,
With ink-stained smiles, they're never used.
They tease the breeze with colors bright,
A painting's chaos, pure delight!

I chase a swirl that takes a spin,
With every slip, my patience thin.
A puddle forms under my shoe,
It splashes ink, oh, what a view!

In gardens wild, we'll laugh and play,
Crafting stories in the sun's ray.
With petals swirling, dancing in sync,
Who knew that nature could be so pink!

The Calligraphy of Seasons

Spring scrawls notes with joyful glee,
While autumn scribbles carelessly.
Each line a twist, a sudden turn,
As leaves make ink, and hearts just yearn.

Summer's laughter writes in gold,
With every ray, a tale unfolds.
It mixes joy, a sunny rhyme,
While winter’s script slows down in time.

The quill's a branch that bends and breaks,
In every stroke, the canvas shakes.
Dialogue with the trees so grand,
Each word a wonder from their hand.

So gather round, let’s take a seat,
To watch the seasons write their beat.
A funny dance in nature’s lore,
Where every whisper opens a door!

Scribbles Beneath the Canopy

With crayons drawn on bark so fine,
The stories wiggle like a vine.
A squirrel pauses, takes a look,
At doodled dreams, not in a book.

The canopy laughs, a leafy jest,
As we create, we feel the zest.
Our laughter spills, a bubbly sound,
While scribbles fly and spin around.

An acorn joins, a doodle’s friend,
In this wild art, there’s no end.
Through tangled vines, our giggles peak,
Nature’s voice helps us to speak.

So let’s embrace this messy quest,
Where every line is quite the jest.
In laughter found beneath the green,
We make our mark, all in between!

Narratives Lost in Translation

A bird once wrote a note and flew,
But it landed where it never knew.
The message read, 'Bring crackers here!'
But they brought a dog—oh dear!

A squirrel tried to send some cheer,
But the stamp was stuck, oh what a leer!
He chased his tail instead of mail,
And laughed at birds that were quite frail.

The fish in ponds had tales to tell,
But spoke in bubbles—oh well, oh well!
They tried to shout, but gurgled deep,
And all they sent was quite a sweep.

So if you wish to send a word,
Make sure it's clear, or you'll be stirred.
A message lost is quite a jest,
But it's the fun that counts, not the rest!

The Palette of Passage

A painter swirled some colors bright,
But mixed the green with brown just right.
He thought he’d painted leaves of spring,
But it looked like mud—a funny ring.

The breeze then whispered, 'What a sight!'
As strange hues danced, out of sheer delight.
A canvas tossed upon the ground,
Made butterflies tumble all around.

While rabbits tried to sketch a hare,
They ended up with blobs, laid bare.
They laughed and hopped with comic flair,
For art is fun when no one's aware!

Oh, nature’s quirks in every shade,
Transforming blunders into a trade.
A riotous splash of wild surprise,
With laughter framed by painted skies!

Scribes of the Natural World

The ants held meetings, oh how they'd plan,
To write a book on life as a clan.
But one spilled ink, and off it went,
Across the ground—oh, what a rent!

The grasshoppers buzzed with fervent glee,
'Let's chronicle this, just wait and see!'
They hopped and skipped to pen their lore,
But the pages flew away—oh, what a chore!

The frogs in midst of nightly croak,
Started scribbling tales, but what a joke!
Their glyphs were more like splashes than text,
A true nature story, but quite perplexed.

So here's to scribes with quirk and writ,
In forests, fields, with every bit.
Their work may not earn a proud display,
But laughter blooms along the way!

Threads of a Gentle Transition

A caterpillar knit a cozy dream,
With threads of sunshine, all agleam.
But forgot to check if it would fit,
Now it's a blanket—what a misfit!

The breeze wove in with a chuckle and sigh,
As flowers giggled, waving bye-bye.
A worm tried to frame his silky line,
But it looked more like a noodle, divine!

The sun pulled strings of warm delight,
While clouds drifted in and out of sight.
They tangled up a fabric bright,
Made patchwork blues, oh what a sight!

Transitions laugh, they twist and twirl,
As nature finds its playful swirl.
So watch the dance with eyes wide open,
In every turn, a jest unbroken!

A Dance of Golden Memories

In a corner, dust bunnies cheer,
Old tales spin like a spinning top,
Nostalgic giggles float in the air,
While the cat takes a snooze, non-stop.

Sunbeams shimmy on the floor,
As shadows play hide and seek,
A sock puppet starts to snore,
With a quirk that's far from meek.

Faded photos tug at smiles,
A mustache drawn on Aunt Sue,
With each frame, a giggle trails,
Who knew that wigs would be so blue?

At dusk, the memories cascade,
Like confetti from a budget show,
Each moment is a laughing parade,
As we dance in the glow of woe.

Fragments of Time's Tapestry

Threads of laughter weave and swirl,
In a quilt of friends and foes,
Tangled yarns make eyebrows curl,
Who knew yarn could go where it goes?

Old clocks tick with silly chimes,
Each second a quirky spin,
As fish absurdly climb the vines,
In a waltz where they all win.

With each stitch, a tale unfolds,
Of epic snacks and questionable rhymes,
A dog in a frog suit, brave and bold,
In a battle for the best of times.

As threads fray and colors clash,
Every knot tells a goofy tale,
In the tapestry, we all smash,
A raucous joy that cannot fail.

Scribe of the Serene

With a quill made from a chicken’s plume,
I write of days that are elephant gray,
Where squirrels in suits promise doom,
In meetings that last all day.

Typed letters dance with glee,
As typos throw a lively fit,
Each errant word, a mystery,
Who knew a cat could be a hit?

Calligraphers with fuzzy hats,
Supplied by tales from sleepy towns,
Where everyone chats with their cats,
And giggles hide beneath the crowns.

So pen down this joyful spree,
As nonsense flies with a happy pace,
In the quiet, there’s quirky glee,
A serene laugh in every space.

The Rustle of Untold Stories

In gardens where giggles grow,
Petunias speak in riddles clear,
A snail claims to be a pro,
At races, but he’s stuck in here.

The breeze tickles fleeting prose,
In corners where shadows play,
Each whisper of nonsense flows,
A kite that took off yesterday.

In the rustle of what’s unsaid,
The crickets plot a daring feat,
With each hop, a rumor spreads,
Who wore the funniest shoes on feet?

So gather round for a laugh or two,
As stories twirl like a silly may,
In the rustle, there’s joy for you,
In the pages of the light of day.

Time's Weathered Manuscript

A squirrel stole my favorite pen,
It wrote a note, but then again,
With acorn ink, it looks quite neat,
Yet all it says is 'Bring me meat.'

The paper crinkled, aged and brown,
With doodles of a silly clown,
I tried to read, but what a shame,
It only scribbles, none the same.

Stanzas of the Forgotten

There once was a tree that did forget,
Its own wise branches, I do bet,
It jotted down a zany thought,
About a cat that couldn't trot.

In gusts of wind, the jokes went far,
With laughter ringing near and far,
Yet twigs just chuckled at the rhymes,
And left the world with silly chimes.

The Poem of the Descending

As whispers swirl around the ground,
A fleeting tale begins to sound,
A tumble, a roll, a playful dance,
A shortsighted bird missed its chance.

It swooped and swayed, oh what a sight,
Then poof! It landed, lost its flight,
Among the giggles of the spry,
It couldn't see the ground nearby.

Tales Written in Nature's Bounty

Upon a napkin, dreams unfold,
Of squirrel scouts all brave and bold,
Their mission brief? To raid the stash,
Of snacks and treats—oh, what a clash!

The acorns roll like tiny balls,
And laughter bounces off the walls,
While ants organize their grand parade,
To steal the crumbs that we all made.

The Alchemy of Transformation

In the garden of giggles, chuckles bloom,
Where colors change faster than a toddler's room.
A butterfly ponders, "Am I still a worm?"
While ants hold a meeting to discuss their firm.

The sun sneezes brightly, a warm, golden spray,
As shadows do jiggles, in a curious way.
A branch winks at a squirrel, who steals the show,
Declaring it’s time for a high-flying throw.

The breeze plays the trumpet, a jazzy sweet tune,
As flowers all whisper, under the moon.
In this wild circus, nature’s a clown,
Doing acrobatics, upside down!

With every small twist, and every new spin,
There’s laughter aplenty, the fun can begin.
Transformations are quirky, like socks on a dog,
In this world of whimsy, let joy be the fog.

Tokens of a Timeworn Journey

A pebble on the road, quite proud of its tale,
Mocks the shiny pebble with a polished sail.
"You think you're so clever, all sparkly and bright,
But I’ve got stories under the moonlight!"

The snail carries wisdom, a library grand,
As he slimes his way through the soft, squishy sand.
"I take my time, mate, hurry’s not for me,
Here’s my wisdom—slow wins the spree!"

A twig draped in laughter cracks jokes all day,
While flowers giggle softly at mischief at play.
“Hey, root, do you hear? That breeze just told a pun!
Nature’s comedy show, oh what fun!”

With each step foraging on this merry stroll,
The world’s a big jester, oh, what a role!
Every rock and each petal remains quite aware,
That in this great journey, humor’s everywhere.

Echoes in the Canopy

In the canopy high, where the giggles reside,
The branches gossip, with leaves as their guide.
"Did you hear that old trunk? It slipped on a root!
He thought he was spry, but fell on his boot!"

The rays of the sun throw a party, it seems,
As shadows dance wildly in whimsical dreams.
Frogs croak out rhymes, and crickets all cheer,
Making sure laughter's the song of the year!

A fruit, oh so juicy, does wobble and roll,
“A gravity check!” says the squirrel on patrol.
The world beneath bursts with chuckles galore,
Even the trees laugh, their laughter a roar!

Echoes resound through the boisterous space,
As nature writes quips with a witty embrace.
In this playful retreat, with joy like confetti,
Every rustle and whisper, a joke that's quite ready.

The Unraveled Scrolls of Nature

An old scroll unravels in the midst of a storm,
A poem of laughter takes vibrant form.
It speaks of a mynah, who learned to recite,
All the cheeky tales that kept her up at night.

The bumblebees buzz with glee on their flight,
As they pollinate blooms with such comic height.
"Hey flower, hold still!" one says with a grin,
"Your pollen's the punchline, let's spread it thin!"

The raindrops join in, a tap-dance so spry,
Racing down petals, oh me, oh my!
A crimson rose chuckles, "I've got quite the scent,
Let's make a perfume of laughter, my friend!"

In nature's grand theater, every scroll tells a tale,
Of quirks and of giggles, of humor set sail.
As whispers unfold under the sun's gentle spell,
The scrolls of the wild ring laughter so well.

Landscapes of the Heart

In the garden of my soul, I'm quite the fool,
Tending to the blooms that laugh, without a rule.
They giggle as they sprout, in colors bold and bright,
Whispering sweet secrets, from morning until night.

With petals clashing colors, like socks gone wrong,
Their vibrant chatter rings out, a funny little song.
A dandelion's dance moves, oh so wild and free,
Make even the most serious, laugh uproariously.

Bouncing bees join in, on joyfully buzzing quests,
While butterflies critique fashion, in their vivid vests.
The sun gives a nod, as it tickles each green head,
In this landscape of my heart, no tears are shed.

In this park of giggles, trust me it's absurd,
Where laughter grows like weeds, yes, it's truly heard.
A fiesta in the field, with each bright little sprout,
The heart wants to be silly, that's what joy's about.

The Cartography of Change

I drew a map of my heart, but it turned out wrong,
The X marks the spot where I lost my thong.
With arrows pointing sideways, directions get bizarre,
I ended up at breakfast instead of the bazaar.

In search of new horizons, I sailed on a whim,
But the compass spun 'round, and the vision went dim.
A salad salad-dressed mystery, tossed in confusion,
And what once was a journey turned into delusion.

Each corner I explore brings an awkward surprise,
Like frogs in my toolbox, with big bulging eyes.
The routes that I wander, full of giggles and glee,
Where change is just a hiccup, not a crisis for me.

With a wink and a nudge, I just go with the flow,
Embracing the twists, like a wiggly show.
This cartography of change, drawn in silly ink,
Maps the joy of my life, don't you dare overthink!

Inkwells of the Wilderness

Inkwells overflow, spilling thoughts everywhere,
Nature's own sticky notes, can you see the flair?
A squirrel stole my pen, now it's scribbling dreams,
While owls watch with bemusement, plotting their schemes.

The brook babbles gossip, a feathered friend's decree,
With ripples of laughter that tickle just beneath.
A bear in a bowtie recites the latest prose,
While panicky rabbits run from the tales that he chose.

The trees quirk their branches, like arms all a-flail,
Grumbling about this year's poetic snail trail.
My quill's got a wild streak, it's drawn to the funk,
Sketching goofy adventures, from the shadows, it's junk.

So in this wild inkwell, where nonsense takes flight,
I chuckle at the chaos, and the creatures that write.
With whimsical spills, and an ink-stained thumb,
The wilderness dances, the laughter is welcome!

Recollections in the Rustle

The whispers of the wind hold secrets from the past,
Tales of clumsy critters, who stumble and outlast.
A worm with a top hat, tiptoes on the breeze,
While the old oak chuckles, shaking all its leaves.

A hedgehog in a tutu twirls under the sun,
Practicing his pirouette, oh what a funny one!
The rustle speaks in riddles, tickling my bright mind,
As memories of frolic become perfectly aligned.

In the chatter of the underbrush, a party starts to brew,
Each sound a silly echo, in this carefree zoo.
And when a breeze comes dancing, the jokes just roll on through,
Each rustle brings a giggle, such hearty hullabaloo!

So come join the laughter, in this whimsical rustle,
Where every leaf is gossip, and we all burst with bustle.
In the memory of nature, let's cause a little cheer,
For in these reflections, we always have a leer.

Messages from Fading Canopies

Beneath a sky of hues so bright,
A squirrel dashed with speed and might.
He dropped a nut, then ran away,
I picked it up, what can I say?

Old branches creaked, they held a tune,
While I danced beneath the smiling moon.
A robin laughed, a feathered peer,
Chirping tales of ancient beer.

The grasses giggled with the breeze,
Telling secrets, if you please.
A paper plane flew by in jest,
Catching whispers, it was the best.

In nature's lounge, where jokes collide,
A leaf forgot it had to hide.
With every rustle, laughter swayed,
In this backyard charade we played.

The Archive of Whispered Colors

In the garden where the colors blend,
A tulip told a joke to a friend.
The daisies roared, the roses blushed,
While violets giggled, thoroughly brushed.

An orange leaf slipped off its branch,
Landed near a dancing ant's prance.
"What's the rush?" the ant inquired,
The leaf just shrugged, "I'm tired, retired!"

The sun stretched wide, yawning in glee,
As petals swayed with utmost glee.
"Did you hear about the sunbeam's fight?"
"Yeah, it lost to the moon last night!"

Winds carrying echoes of fun,
Nature's choir, a lively run.
An archive filled with laughter's glow,
Where petals tell tales of long ago.

Ballads of the Wandering Wind

Oh, the wind sings with a cheeky sound,
Carrying stories from the ground.
A butterfly caught in a silly whirl,
Proclaimed herself the twirling girl.

With each gust, a tickle so light,
The trees giggled, feeling alright.
A bashful branch waved to a bee,
“Come here, let’s sip sweet harmony!”

Clouds passed by with a mischievous glee,
Spoiling the sun for you and me.
"Why so shy?" the raindrops jeered,
"Come dance with us! Be not afeared!"

In the vast embrace where laughter blends,
The wandering whispers are good friends.
Each puff a tale, each rustle a grin,
Come join the ballad, let the fun begin!

Poetry Encased in Arbor

Beneath the boughs where shadows play,
A witty chipmunk stole the day.
He juggled acorns with flair and style,
Winning laughs all the while.

The bark held wisdom in each line,
While beetles plotted, sipping brine.
"What’s a tree’s favorite kind of snack?"
"Bark-becue, with a side of crack!"

Amidst the roots where secrets dwell,
Laughter echoes, a joyful bell.
An oak chuckled, “I’m not so grand,
But I can still provide a hand!”

So gather round in nature’s store,
Where every branch tells tales galore.
Poems and punchlines intertwined,
In this wooded whimsy, joy you'll find.

Rustling Tales of Old

In the garden where whispers play,
A squirrel took my sandwich away.
He paused for a moment, looked quite chummy,
As if to say, "This meal’s too yummy!"

A butterfly danced, trying to show,
How to juggle with seeds in tow.
It landed on my nose for fun,
And there we laughed under the sun.

A breeze poked me with icy fingers,
As if to say, 'Do you have any zingers?'
I told it a joke, 'What do you think?'
The trees all chuckled, I swear they winked!

So I sat among those playful pals,
Where every chirp and rustle calls.
A tale of giggles among the green,
A captivation, quite unforeseen.

The Map of a Quiet Journey

A compass maps the route of giggles,
Through fields where nature quietly wiggles.
I found a sign that read, 'Detour Here,'
But it pointed to a pie shop, oh dear!

The ants had formed a rowdy parade,
With tiny hats and plans well laid.
They brushed past me with grand desires,
To steal the lunch, while chasing fires!

Breezes whispered jokes in my ear,
About a cloud who lost a rear.
He floated off, held up by dreams,
While I chased blooms, or so it seems.

And as I wandered without a care,
The sun peeked through with a golden flare.
In the laughter of flowers, I found delight,
This map was quirky, but felt so right.

Emotions Framed in Gold

A daisy told me tales of woe,
Lost in thought, just chasing tow.
The wind then chimed in with a twist,
Saying, "Bloom where you think you missed!"

I saw a heart-shaped potato grin,
Won a contest, with a cheeky spin.
It danced around, stole the show,
Bragged about the best baked glow!

The sun blushed red, feeling quite proud,
As shadows formed a goofy crowd.
I giggled, wishing to capture the cheer,
With photos and memories, oh so dear.

A frame of joy with colors bright,
Each moment caught in playful light.
In this gallery of nature’s art,
Every giggle warms the heart.

Nature's Unwritten Verses

Underneath the quirky boughs,
A frog recites its unwritten vows.
It croaks of hopes, both wild and bold,
A riot of dreams yet to unfold.

The moon chuckled, with a twinkle or two,
Saying, “You humans haven't a clue!”
While snails lined up for a slow dance,
It seemed they had quite the chance!

The trees began their funny sway,
Echoing secrets of yesterday.
With every chime of nature's jive,
I felt like the silliest alive.

So here’s to verses in fields untried,
Where laughter and whimsy do abide.
In the wild, it’s all a quirky spree,
Nature’s jokes are meant to be free!

Harvesting Memories from the Wind

When breezes whisper secrets true,
Old jokes take flight like birds on cue.
I chase them down, they spin and twirl,
Each one a giggle, a joyful swirl.

Like fruit that falls from trees above,
I gather stories, sprinkle love.
With every gust, laughter grows,
In windswept fields, my humor flows.

A hat flung high, a shoe that flies,
I catch them both with goofy sighs.
The dance of nature, a silly jest,
In every gust, a chuckle's best.

So when the autumn starts to play,
I'll harvest laughter, come what may.
With every rustle, joy appears,
A tree of laughter through the years.

Conversations in Color

A crimson chat beneath the sun,
Where shades of laughter make it fun.
The yellow laughs, the green retorts,
They argue softly, hold court in sports.

Orange spills jokes like juice in cups,
While blue rolls eyes and never erupts.
Together they paint a tale absurd,
In a language only nature heard.

Purple grins, saying life is bright,
As pink adds flair with all its might.
In this rib-tickling, colorful show,
They trade wisecracks and playful flow.

So take a seat, enjoy the spree,
In this palette of glee, there’s no fee.
For when the hues start to collide,
The laughter's vibrant, a joyful ride.

The Signature of Seasons

Spring scribbles poems, cheeky and light,
While summer bursts forth, oh what a sight!
Autumn drafts letters, crisp and neat,
And winter just lingers, with chill in retreat.

With each changing page, the world’s a play,
Where puns are penned in the sun's bright ray.
Snowflakes giggle as they drift and twirl,
While raindrops chuckle, a graceful whirl.

Leaves that flutter, a signature fine,
Dance like clowns on a bright sunny line.
With every shift, a jest unfolds,
In nature’s library, the laughter holds.

So flip through the chapters, take a glance,
In the book of seasons, join the dance.
With whimsical squiggles, they play their part,
Nature’s schtick, it's a playful art.

Fragments in the Wind

Bits of chatter float through the air,
Like paper airplanes without a care.
They spiral up and tumble down,
Making silly faces, wearing a frown.

Laughter logs ride on the breeze,
Spreading humor, aiming to please.
Squirrels read bits in a comical stance,
In the wind's embrace, they twist and prance.

A tiny bit of gossip zooms,
As nature's jesters claim the rooms.
Each fragment collects the giggles and sighs,
In the airy dance, where fun never dies.

So listen close for the wind's delight,
Where whispers of whimsy take flight.
In every breath, find a joyful spin,
Collecting fragments caught in the wind.

An Anthology of Earth’s Whisper

In a breeze the stories dance,
Nature giggles in its chance.
Paper dreams come out to play,
Whispering secrets, come what may.

Scribbles fine, some wobbly too,
A laugh from a tree, is that you?
Ticklish twigs in a cheerful bout,
Echoing laughter, what’s it about?

Rolling around, a smooth little stone,
Snickering softly, never alone.
A playful toss with a nutty grin,
In this wacky world, let the fun begin!

With such folly around the bend,
Every swirl and twist, a new trend.
Nature's confetti, swirling with glee,
Tickling our hearts, wild and free.

Subtle Signatures on the Ground

An acorn winks with a sly delight,
While dandelions plot through the night.
Footprints scatter, a playful trace,
Nature's mime in this comical space.

A wiggly worm does a funky dance,
Rocking the soil like it's a chance.
Mud pies flying in joyous cheer,
Can you spot the squirrel sneer?

As puddles reflect a jolly spree,
Frogs croak in their own symphony.
With every stomp, the joy spills out,
Turning the ground into a shout!

So step with glee, embrace the fun,
With every prank, our hearts are spun.
Nature's canvas, a cheerful sight,
Where laughter blooms from day to night.

The Story of Soft Crinkles

In the breeze, they flap and jig,
Each little fold, a lively gig.
Crunchy whispers, tickling ears,
Nature’s riddle, sparking cheers.

Like crumbling cookies, they scatter wide,
As squirrels frolic, full of pride.
Every wrinkle tells a jest,
Nature’s humor, at its best!

A paper trail of glimmers bright,
Each crease a chuckle in soft twilight.
Giggles arise with each stomp and shuffle,
In this joyful world, there’s never a scuffle.

So gather ‘round, hear the laughs unfold,
With stories sprouting, brave and bold.
A tale of crinkles, a playful sound,
In every corner, fun is found.

Memories Captured in Graphite

Sketches made by nature's hand,
Giggles sketched across the land.
Pencils twirl with such delight,
As sketchy characters take to flight.

With every swirl, a tale spins round,
Jolly instances are tightly bound.
Highlights dance in shimmery fun,
Each shade a laughter, never done.

A scribble here, a doodle there,
The cheeky critters start to glare.
Sketchbooks filled with whirls of glee,
Nature draws out the light-hearted spree!

From dusk till dawn, let’s trace the beat,
In graphite laughter, we find our seat.
Erasers chuckle, keeping score,
As joy spills out from every drawer.

The Diary of Rust and Gold

Once I found a shiny note,
Tucked beneath a spider's coat.
It told me secrets of the sun,
And how to dance while on the run.

Crinkled pages, wild and torn,
With tales of creatures, never worn.
A squirrel wrote in hasty scrawl,
About that time he took a fall.

The ink was spilled with acorn juice,
A nutty tale, oh what a hoot!
Each line a giggle, every word a cheer,
I laughed so hard, I spilled my beer.

So next time nature's swirls unfold,
Check for stories, brave and bold.
For every wrinkle hides a jest,
In the diary of rust and gold.

Sentences Carried by the Current

A rubber ducky drifts downstream,
With messages that make you beam.
“Quack your way to fun and play!”
The current hums a silly lay.

Papers swirl in watery dance,
Each one hoping to get a chance.
A fishy phrase, a slimy pun,
Turns an average day to fun.

“Watch out for the splashes!” they say,
“Or your picnic's plans might go astray!”
Bubbles carry a chortled cheer,
As laughter floats, it’s very clear.

So if you find a soggy tale,
Just grab a boat, and set your sail.
For sentences that ride the flow,
Bring smiles wherever they go.

The Stanzas of a Rustic Path

Upon a trail of muddy bliss,
A wise old sign claims, “Don’t you miss!
The path that zigzags like your sock,
Each twist and turn, a funny knock.”

The daisies wink with purple hues,
As gnarly roots wear nature’s shoes.
“Oh don’t trip here! You’ll lose your hat!”
Cries a squirrel with a cheeky spat.

A wandering snail with a speckled shell,
Thought he'd write but tripped and fell.
His notes became a squiggled smear,
An artful mess, we hold so dear.

So walk the path, embrace the twist,
Where laughter hides in morning mist.
Each step a joke, a giggly laugh,
On this rustic path, do take a gaff!

Scribes of the Whispering Woods

In the trees where whispers bloom,
A rabbit shares his penned-up gloom.
With carrots lined like little stars,
He scratches poems from afar.

“Dear friends, your veggies won’t betray,
If you just hop and munch all day!”
The forest chuckles with its cheer,
As leafy quills create good beer.

A turtle in his ancient shell,
Wrote tales of slow—the best of sell.
With every line, he earned a grin,
Slowpoke wisdom, all within.

So join the scribes, let laughter ring,
In the woods where all creatures sing.
For every tale spins a funny twist,
In a world where joy should persist.

Pages Danced by Flickering Light

In the glow of the lamp, a page takes flight,
Giggles of ink, dancing through the night.
A scribble escapes, a mischievous sprite,
Taking jests at the pen, a comical sight.

Footnotes trip over, plotting their schemes,
Margins are laughing, bursting at seams.
Each curl of the script has its own little dreams,
As laughter erupts from the paper it beams.

The author awakes, with a puzzled grin,
Wondering how this chaos could begin.
But the jesters rejoice, and they twirl and spin,
In the margins of madness, they're ready to win!

So let it be known, in the story that's told,
Words have a spirit, and they're surprisingly bold.
With a flicker of light, their antics unfold,
As the pages unite in a giggle of gold.

The Scripted Embrace of Change

Doodles in ink, writing history's quirks,
Each paradox laughing as it subtly lurks.
Chapters like chameleons, slipping with smirks,
Carrying jokes, like mischievous sparks.

A tale once serious, now takes a twist,
Characters stumble; their plans go amiss.
Plot holes are giggling, no way they resist,
As footnotes conspire, embracing the mist.

The pen tries to follow, but falls far behind,
While the ideas break loose, leaving confusion blind.
Plot bunnies are hopping, with tales intertwined,
The scripted embrace, with hilarity combined.

So turn the next page, let the nonsense commence,
Where riddles and ramblings are thick with suspense.
In the theater of writing, an uproarious fence,
Holds laughter aplenty, and absurd recompense.

Tales Woven in Nature's Tapestry.

Breezes are whispering, secrets they share,
Spinning yarns thick with laughter and flair.
A tree's friendly branches wave right through the air,
Teasing the critters who scamper with care.

Sunlight and shadows play peek-a-boo fun,
While ants in their suits march, thinking they've won.
"Who's the big boss?" chirps a ladybird spun,
But the answer is tangled—nature's just begun!

Clouds roll in giggles, dressed up for a show,
Taking bets on how fast they'll grow.
Raindrops are winking, with each joyous flow,
Splashing in puddles, feeling the glow.

So gather the stories, let laughter entwine,
From blossoms to beetles, in sunlight they shine.
Nature's a comedian, in layers so fine,
Weaving tales of joy, like a funny design.

Whispers of the Falling

As the wind starts to chuckle, it tickles the trees,
Falling from branches, they spiral with ease.
The ground catches laughter in rustling pleas,
Where nature throws parties, inviting the breeze.

Each tumble is troublesome, a comedic flair,
Creating a ruckus without any care.
Marigolds giggle, caught in mid-air,
As the world spins beneath them, a carnival fair.

Squirrels are prancing, preparing a feast,
With acorns a-falling, what fun at least!
“Oops, dropped my snack!” says a bird with a tweet,
As nature’s own circus plays out in the street.

So join in the fun, as the world starts to sway,
With each little whisper, let laughter play.
Falling from high, with a humorous display,
Where giggles are caught and carried away.

Epistles in the Orchard

In the orchard, fruits confer,
With apples typing on their spur.
Pears giggle as they drop and roll,
Witty notes of sweet control.

A banana slips on sunny paths,
While cherries craft the silliest laughs.
Behind the trunk, a grape lays low,
And drafts a tale of woe in flow.

A round peach pranks a sly old plum,
As oranges watch, they hum and strum.
'Let's share our juice!' the berries cry,
While nuts just sigh, 'We're born to dry!'

So gather round, this fruity crew,
With humor, juice, and gossip too.
In knots and strings of jests they weave,
An orchard's life is one to cleave!

The Colors of Change

A riot at the forest floor,
Where yellows dance and reds explore.
Orange critters tease the green,
While sassafras holds court, unseen.

Purple twigs do cha-cha slide,
As golden leaves take autumn's ride.
'Who stole my color?' one branch says,
A magenta joke makes nature's plays.

A rusty acorn drops with flair,
"I'm changing; catch me if you dare!"
The vibrant squabble turns to glee,
As hues collide in jubilee.

So grab your pals and join the scene,
Where every shade can be serene.
In nature's palette, fun abounds,
In laughter's echo, joy resounds!

Transcripts of an Ancient Tree

Beneath the bark, a chronicle lies,
Of squirrels swiping nuts and pies.
“From year to year, we’ve had our fun!”
Scribbled tales of rain and sun.

The owl, a witness, always hoots,
To shenanigans of tiny roots.
“Remember when the storm took flight?
And we banded ‘round, all through the night?”

Inky spiders spin in jest,
As branches boast of their best test.
“No tree can tangle like my roots,
Or claim them all in furry suits!”

So grab a bark and join the fray,
With giggles echoing the day.
An ancient tree can tell it all,
In stories thick as winter's pall!

Messages in the Breeze

A ticklish wind sends whispers round,
Each gust delivers funny sound.
“Hey leaf, you’re flying just like me!”
Cried one to the dandelion's spree.

Pine needles laugh at woven tales,
While graceful winds share silly gales.
“What’s that up there? A hat? A shoe?”
As butterflies spin in swirls anew.

A tumbleweed with puns in tow,
Rolls over hills, just puts on a show.
“Catch that breeze—don’t let it flee!”
Said the fern to gossiping brie.

So sail along, let laughter steer,
The wind brings messages quite clear.
In nature’s jest, delight unfurls,
As breezy chuckles rock the world!

Harvesting Echoes

A fluttering note flew straight to my nose,
It tickled and sneezed, what a silly pose!
I gathered the whispers from branches so spry,
They giggled and danced as they waved goodbye.

An acorn chuckled, 'I’ll never be a tree!'
While a squirrel proclaimed, 'Just wait and see!'
They pranced in a circle, a forest parade,
With winks and with nods, their vows were made.

Banana peels laughed at their fruity plight,
'We're slippery jesters, just adding to the fright!'
They slipped on their own tails, oh what a scene,
Nature's own comedy, a vibrant routine.

And though all may fall as the harvest does call,
Each giggle and prank should be cherished by all.
So gather your chuckles beneath trees on high,
For laughter's the bounty that never says die.

The Poetry of Decay

Oh, the tales of the ground, where the old stuff rots,
Each withered petal has stories, you’ve got!
Mushrooms write ballads, sprouting in style,
While worms recite sonnets that stretch for a mile.

A rusty tin can sings its metallic tune,
'The world spins round, like a silly balloon!'
With beetles as dancers and ants in the mix,
It's a raucous review in the composting fix.

The apples sing soft, 'We’re past our prime,'
With soft, squishy lines, a real slippery rhyme.
And yet, little seeds, they dream in the muck,
Of green days ahead, ‘cause they’ve all got luck!

In the grunge of decay, life thrives and confides,
With humor and charm, the old still abides.
So don’t scorn the past, for its secrets stay dear,
With laughter and wisdom, we all persevere.

Sentiments on the Soft Earth

Beneath the ground, where the critters all dwell,
Are whispers of secrets, both funny and swell.
A potato giggles, 'I'll turn into fries!'
As chubby little roots make jokes 'neath the skies.

The dirt said, 'Hey! I'm more than just grime!'
'I've got worms telling stories, all in good time!'
The sun tickles grass, that tickles the breeze,
While toads croak their curses with giggles and wheeze.

A dandelion's dream is to be a bouquet,
But ends up in salad; oh, what a cliché!
Yet every fine sprout with its patchwork attire,
Reminds us that growth is a comedic fire.

So dance on the soil, spread your giggles and cheer,
For nature's punchlines are loud and quite clear.
Under the surface, where laughter takes root,
There's joy in the journey; don't leave it to brood!

Inscriptions of the Forest Floor

Beneath old pine trees, where the shadows do play,
Lies the diary of nature written in hay.
A squirrel doodles with acorns and twigs,
While bunnies do yoga, striking their gigs.

Insects etch tales on the bark of the trees,
With puns about pollen and hummingbird fees.
The moss mocks the daisies, 'You're just too pristine!'
While brambles throw parties, their thorns just unseen.

'Look at me roll!' cried a beetle with flair,
As he wobbled and tumbled, no shame in the air.
'Life's one big joke, just try not to pout,'
With the laughter of critters that never run out.

So next time you wander through forests so deep,
Remember their stories and laughter they keep.
For every twig whispers a joyfully penned,
Inscriptions of humor that never will end.

Pages Adrift on Autumn's Breath

In a fluttering dance, they spin and twirl,
Whirling like paper in a playful whirl.
Each twist a giggle, each turn a skit,
Nature's own jest, a colorful hit.

They slide on sidewalks, a raucous laugh,
Pretending to sail on a watercraft.
Stuck to shoes, they role-play a team,
Pirates of fall with a giggly gleam.

From branches they tumble, wearing a crown,
A patchwork of laughter, tumbling down.
An army of chuckles on the ground waits,
With whispers of fun that nobody states.

Oh, have you seen the comic parade?
As they rush off, plans hastily made.
Notes of cheer in the crisp, cool air,
With every shuffle, a new joke to share.

Nature's Written Symphony

Twirling lines in the gentle breeze,
Chasing giggles with the greatest ease.
A playful rhythm, a cheeky beat,
Nature's voice makes the funny sweet.

Scribbled notes on the wind's loud calls,
Echoing laughter through tree-lined halls.
With each rustle, a joke takes flight,
In the symphony of day and night.

Whispers collide in a lightweight tease,
As branches conspire with gradual ease.
A comedy skit on the forest floor,
Where smiles abound and giggles encore.

With scribbles of charm in colors bright,
They dance in circles, pure delight.
Harmonized mischief surrounds the day,
It's a quirky show in an outdoors play.

Rustling Tales in the Breeze

Once upon a time in a golden mop,
A tale arose with a playful hop.
Rustling whispers cast out the spell,
Of silly stories we all know so well.

An acorn's a jewel in a leaf-styled crown,
With squirrels narrating their comic frown.
Puppets of nature, each proud to tell,
Of memos misplaced that went very swell.

Tales of adventures, absurd yet true,
Of jigsaw patches in a trendy hue.
As breezes giggle, the drama unfolds,
With every rustle, a secret retold.

So lean in closer, listen with glee,
To the gossiping wind, it's all just for free.
Each twig a witness to funniness framed,
In the rustling tales, the laughter's unclaimed.

The Script of Falling Colors

Written in colors, a comic script,
On branches and breezes, it wonderfully slipped.
Falling like laughter from the trees high,
A colorful banquet beneath the sky.

The plot thickens at the season's start,
With reds and yellows wearing each heart.
Comic relief in a whirl of shades,
As jokes from the treetops are steadily laid.

Dancing about, both silly and bright,
The script unfolds, a hilarious sight.
Nature’s own giggles adorn the ground,
In this vivid play, joy can be found.

So when you glance at the swirling spree,
Know life’s just a jest, wild and free.
With each falling piece, a chuckle escapes,
In the theater of foliage, joy reshapes.

www.ingramcontent.com/pod-product-compliance
Lightning Source LLC
Chambersburg PA
CBHW070319120526
44590CB00017B/2741
9781805814269